HALF PINT EDITIONS

JUST CATS

TEXT BY KAREN ANDERSON

WILLOW CREEK PRESS

Minocqua, Wisconsin

Published by WILLOW CREEK PRESS, INC.

PO Box 147, Minocqua, WI 54548

For more information on Willow Creek Press titles, call 1-800-850-9453.

Library of Congress Cataloging-in-Publication Data

Anderson, Karen.

    Just cats / text by Karen Anderson. -- Half pint ed.

        p.   cm.

    ISBN 1-57223-220-X

    1. Cats.   2. Cats--Pictorial works.

3. Photography of cats. I. Title.

SF442.A536   1999

636.8--dc21   98-52369

                                 CIP

Printed in Canada.

CONTENTS

PORTRAITS

Behold the Cat

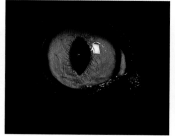

The cat. The *felis catus*. Wild, unpredictable, self-sufficient. And this is the domestic cat we're talking about! Though cats began hanging around humans at least 3,000 years ago, you often wouldn't know it. To a fascinating degree, many of the ancestral traits of the European and African wild cats have become only slightly tempered in the domestic cats of today, presenting us with a glorious, privileged peek into the eyes of a very natural, largely unspoiled creature.

Portraits

Just Cats

A nd what piercing, penetrating, eyes they are — as if each discerning eyeball peers right into your very soul. There's not much you can hide from a cat; they just seem to intuitively *know* what we're really about. They also sense who are the "cat people" and who aren't . . . a nice bit of information to obtain if you're a cat.

Just Cats

Cats manage to command our attention without even trying. There sits the feline, so quietly and stunningly beautiful, neither demanding nor outrightly asking for our gaze, yet receiving it just the same! We can hardly resist connecting with a cat; the experience is at once mesmerizing, exhilarating, even humbling. Little wonder the ancient Egyptians literally *worshipped* cats!

Portraits

Just Cats

Portraits

Cats use their whole bodies to communicate. There's the "come hither" look, the "scratch me please" gesture or the "I-know-you-really-do-want-to-play-even-though-you-think-you're-too-busy" position.

Sometime since the late 1880s, when keeping cats as pets caught on in the U.S. with fervor, the cat has officially found its way into more homes than the pet dog . . . and it shows no signs of relinquishing that honor. These days people are discovering renewed, dramatic interest in cats and in understanding and appreciating the feline. After a rocky history and an unwarranted suspect past, cats are finally getting the kind of honest, balanced publicity they deserve.

Just Cats

Portraits

Just Cats

Regardless of the hand dealt a particular cat, each one retains its unmistakable feline dignity; making the absolute best of his situation and figuring out how to make life work — and work *well*. That cats are confident is a vast understatement. They pride themselves on their ability to cope, to endure, to thrive.

Portraits

Just Cats

An innate, natural elegance permeates everything the feline does, from lounging upon the ground, to careful grooming, to speaking up. There is something ethereal about cats . . . yet so real indeed. They are objects of art come to life.

The question is, do they know it? They are surely aware of their attractiveness and take great care in their upkeep, but it's doubtful they grasp just how sublime their entire appearance actually is. (And that's probably a good thing.)

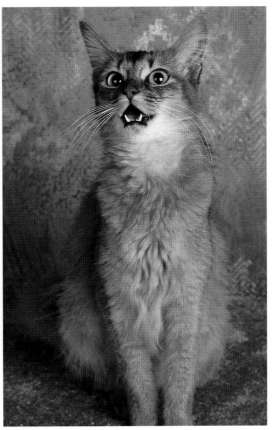

Portraits

Country Cats

Land of Opportunity

This is how it starts: Tabby is acting shy and secretive. She's hanging out around the barn . . . what is she doing behind the hay bales? You investigate and — *voila!* — the farm's cat population has increased eightfold. Country life for these contented little tykes promises to be about as exciting as it gets for domestic felines in our world today.

There's a big, undiscovered universe outside the barn and in no time the kittens will get the chance to explore their options. If a farm has any cats at all, it most likely houses several cats or even dozens. Littermates and their cousins mingle and mix, producing all sorts of hearty stock.

Just Cats

Country Cats

I nquiring minds want to know. Or at least get
close enough to be amused. A cat's natural
curiosity serves it well on the farm and is a sure
boredom-buster on any given day. Cats love to get
into things . . . get up onto things . . . go over
things . . . and go under things. There is positively
no end to fascinating kitty adventures!

Just Cats

Country Cats

On the farm, kittens are able to highly develop their traditional hunting skills. For one thing, the ratio of mice to cats is in the cats' favor. Most farm cats are master mousers. Meaningful mousehunt moments abound in the fields, among the tall grasses and in the corners of the barn. Small rodents of all sorts, including voles, shrews — even grasshoppers — are considered by kitty to be quite a prize.

Unfortunately, there are an awful lot of sweet songbirds and backyard feathered friends who meet their end when a feline is near. Some cats hunt the hapless birds for dinner, while others merely find their stunt flying a challenge and chase the birds for sport. As turned-off as we might become over such unseemly pursuits, it does no good to rebuke the clever feline attacker — the cat is merely acting on firmly entrenched instincts that aren't going away anytime soon.

Country Cats

Just Cats

A cat's body is perfectly outfitted for hunting and the drama of daily living. Rural cats get to regularly hone their amazing physical skills and put them to proper use. The marvelously flexible spine permits the cat to bend, twist, leap and land with ease and gracefulness. Its exceedingly strong hind legs are what thrusts it into the air (up to five times its height) or onto prey. With perfect, powerful poise a long, wafting tail helps to maintain the cat's balance wherever its padded feet take it.

Country Cats

Just Cats

C ountry livin' is mighty fine — at least most of the time. A cat who lives away from the city with lots of space to explore and land to acquire has amenities and opportunities that city cats only dream of. Rugged farm cats enjoy a rough-and-ready self-reliance that breeds an air of easy confidence unique to cats of the countryside.

Just Cats

Farm cats are certainly prolific but still precious, every one. Happily for the rural cat community, more and more country cat owners are beginning to resist the notion that farm cats are a replaceable commodity and are watching out for their safety, medical needs and general well-being more closely.

Country Cats

Just Cats

Country Cats

I n the country, there are treats and treasures galore. Cats get the run of the place, with acres upon acres to hunt and discover. Sips of fresh dairy milk are just a cow away. There are infinite spots to cozily nap and no lack of activity and entertainment to engage in firsthand or monitor from a convenient window.

Just Cats

Country Cats

Especially brought to life on a farm, one of the great hallmarks of the feline is its indomitable independent spirit. However, one could just as accurately describe a cat as positively *de*pendent! Truly, the domestic cat seems to be something of a paradox. It freely accepts human attention and companionship on the one hand, yet never allows even the most comfy life to diminish the cat's sense of who he is and what he is perfectly capable of.

Country cats are pretty much self-governing and can wander off for hours at a time, but very little will keep them from enjoying special times with their people. A cuddle, a chat, a bowl of milk from loving hands . . . and still the master of their days. Now *this* is living the high life!

Just Cats

Country Cats

Suburban Cats

The Best of Both Worlds

Suburban cats are similar to their country cousins in that they spend their time in and around the house; only the property is measured in parklike square feet rather than rambling acres.

A quiet, meandering neighborhood is a pretty decent place to raise a cat. Usually, there's a fair amount of yard and garden to wander through, endless indoor gymnastic pursuits and plenty of accommodating perches from which to survey anything and everything.

Just Cats

Suburban Cats

Suburbia being more sedate than the wild countryside, the cats who live there are accordingly more refined and reserved. You could say that these cats have got life a bit easy . . . with less need to hunt for meals and more time to kick back.

And they do so much for the landscape! Whether they're sitting somewhere as a feline finial or stretched out gracefully across a bench, it cannot be ignored that cats beautify and enhance the planet. To be sure, these striking, ever-changing, living garden ornaments can rival even the most handsome stone sculptures!

Just Cats

Suburban Cats

Just Cats

E ven in the 'burbs, enterprising cats will find fresh-mown lawn to run and tumble on and useful trees — or even houses — to climb. Kitty patrols her territory continuously; diligently inspecting for signs of visitors and perhaps watching for the return of a beloved human companion.

One can't be certain just where the cat will turn up and just what she might be doing. It's not uncommon to be going about the day's business and then spot a cat spying on *you*.

Suburban Cats

Perky the dog is testing the patience of Princess the cat. Why do some dogs insist on antagonizing cats, anyway? To a dog it's merely a game where pooch frightens the cat enough to send it running, which then provides the (usually bored) dog with a fast-moving critter to chase. Kitty is entirely offended however, and will either graphically demonstrate to the canine how her claws work . . . or sprint at speeds of nearly 30 mph to flee the pesky puppy.

Suburban Cats

Just Cats

U nless cats are asleep, they most *always* seem to be on the watch. What may look to be mindless observation by the cat is usually nothing short of a thorough information-gathering exercise. Combine their impressive sense of smell, their acutely sensitive ears and their keen vision and you've got one highly sophisticated creature . . . suitable for the most delicate intelligence missions.

Cats are easily amused by life. They will trace the fall of a leaf, follow the movements of a moth, stare endlessly at a fellow feline or gaze into the distance with who-knows-what on his mind. Then again, the cat may just hunker down among the vegetation and watch the world go by.

Suburban Cats

A special benefit of suburban living is the close proximity of people. Cats are incredible — here they are one short leap from their untamed roots and yet clearly pursuing relationships with us. It's not that they need us, per se: they *want* us.

Just Cats

When a cat permits a stroke down its back or a scratch behind the ears we cannot help but feel we've been somehow accepted into the inner circle of an elite group. It feels like a great privilege to be *that* near a cat. Maybe it's the very fact that the feline can (and often does) move through life so superbly without human intervention that we experience such gratitude at being allowed to become intimate with a cat and meaningfully contribute to its life. After all, we've been told for years how independent cats are!

Suburban Cats

CITY CATS

The Prince and the Pauper

The city can be a dangerous place for a cat . . . particularly a lost one. Homelessness in the city is not unique to humans. Cats are so adaptable that strays wandering through city streets are common. Usually, the cats we see darting in and out of alleyways don't belong to anyone; they are wild or feral cats who make their homes in the urban jungle.

Without grassy fields, garden hide-outs and quiet nooks for safe snoozing, cats in the city are left to eke out an existence amid concrete and steel. They get used to all of this (most have known little else) and of course make the best of it, but it's a bittersweet scene nonetheless.

Just Cats

City Cats

Just Cats

C ats who live in urban settings are real survivors — they have to be. City felines are streetwise from the get-go and find themselves in fierce competition for food and territory. As street cats know well enough, there are only so many cafe dumpsters and unclaimed bits of paved "land" to go around.

These lucky ones have found work in retail — how about a secure, upstanding career in window dressing or store management ?

City Cats

Just Cats

T hankfully, not all cats who dwell in the city limits are on their own. Lots of urbanites come home daily to a human family and find their niche in or around the house — contentedly settling in with savvy and decorum. Some city cats, like these Key West residents, live relatively "normal" lives with plenty of exposure to the outdoors.

City Cats

But for reasons of safety and practicality, most city cats are shut-ins. This is not to say that quality of life within the confines of a home is necessarily poor! Provided the cat has the run of the place and loving friends, kitty will do just fine. Actually, a good many cosmopolitan cats lead the most privileged and pampered existence of the lot — compromising outdoor freedoms for the tranquillity of mighty cushy digs. Don't feel *too* sorry for them.

City Cats

Just Cats

It goes without saying, however, that cats who spend all day and night inside a carefully controlled environment do need extra excitement built into their days. It's okay to be stuck on the inside looking out, as long as someone on the inside is intent on keeping life interesting for you. Even the chance to get a whiff of the outside air or soak up a few minutes of sun is relished by a full-time housecat and goes a long way to break up the day.

City Cats

Just Cats

Some city cats live in a proverbial bubble and remain blissfully unaware of the throb of the city below. With pizzazz and panache, these well-nurtured felines grace the condos and apartments deep in the heart of town. Cramped as they are in their protected palaces, they seem to thrive quite well in the restricted world, claiming every inch, every nook and cranny as their own.

City Cats

Just Cats

K itty thinks this vase of fresh flowers is great to play with no matter *what* those sticks-in-the-mud people have to say about it (and they aren't home anyway). Hey, sometimes a cat has to get imaginative and creatively seek avenues for his own fun! It's quite a sight to stumble upon a cat frolicking unabashedly, be it tracking a wind-up mouse, discovering how splendid wicker can be for claw sharpening or putting otherwise mundane household gadgets to good use.

City Cats

Just Cats

City Cats

I ndoor cats love to practice and enjoy their prized hunting skills . . . even if the only varmint the cat will ever meet is a fake little toy. Almost any SMO (small moving object) works nicely as kitty pretends it's the real thing — tossing it to and fro and hiding it from himself purposely to prolong the game.

Every single day at one time or another, the feline is in pursuit of *something*. It's just that a few dipping, darting, fluttery little pip-squeaks are harder to get to than others.

City Cats

Just Cats

C ity cats tend to be well-groomed, refined and studious. They put a little more energy into how they look and are granted many fine opportunities for cultivating good taste and aesthetic values.

City Cats

Of course cats will be cats no matter where they live — and you won't have to guess when kitty has a strong opinion about something. City cats are usually open to new and different cuisine; yet curiously intolerant of new brands of kitty litter.

Just Cats

City Cats

Just Cats

R egardless of the worldly esca-
pades that cats enjoy, it's the
human housemates they become
particularly fond of. Cats *do* come
down off the roofs, around the corners,
through the doorways, off the window
sills and onto our laps. At the end of a
full and varied day, as long as kitty
knows she is astonishingly adored and
impeccably loved, all seems right with
the world.

City Cats

Kittens

The Way They Were

It doesn't matter what age you are when a new kitten comes into your life . . . the event is always a heart-melting experience. Cats enter our lives with the idea the relationship is going to last for a long, long time. They don't necessarily rush into friendship (although cats can sense a cat devotee quicker than you can say "cat-got-your-tongue?"), but once the real deal comes their way, cats will shamelessly wrap themselves around your heart just as their tails twine around your legs.

We knew this intuitively long before the research commenced, but study after study has proven that people who share their home with a pet (specifically cats and dogs) are less stressed. Anxiety levels drop dramatically when we begin nurturing a pet. With cats especially, their presence soothes, inspires and relaxes. Bring on the cats!

Just Cats

Kittens

Just Cats

There is nothing like a dear little batch of kittens to brighten one's day. These little tykes are so funny, so sweet, so curious, so charmingly awkward and unsure. You look at a young kitten and have to wonder how these squirmy, fluffy balls of frivolity ever metamorphosize into sleek, elegant adult cats! Of course they always do — over the course of a few short months —

and this journey to adulthood is marvelously fun to watch.

At first the tiny, snuggling newborns stay right at mom's side just nursing and sleeping . . . totally dependent upon mama cat. By the time they are eight or nine weeks old the wiggly kittens are totally weaned, feasting on all sorts of newfound nibbles, and are well on their way to considering *you* their primary source for nutritional and emotional nourishment.

A kitten's world gets bigger and bigger, wider and wider as the weeks march on. Soon you'll start to see their adorable sniffing noses inch further and further from mom and bravely tiptoeing into the great unknown. The picture of innocence, kittens can be paired with any number of similarly defenseless critters.

Just Cats

Kittens

Just Cats

B ut it isn't long before you notice suspicious changes in kitty: an intensity of the eyes you hadn't before recognized; a tendency to study things from a hiding place; and good heavens, kitty's now stalking that poor bunny . . . with evil intent!

Kittens

K ittens love to play and seem to positively live for it. Besides sporting with bugs, leaves, cat toys and other fascinating found objects, kittens find immense pleasure in playing with each other. They will chase, wrestle and roll amidst a tumble of tails, paws and downy fur. As well as exercising some of their hunting instincts, the raucous and rowdy kittens are also learning to fight for what they want. Sweet, gentle brotherly or sisterly play can turn a bit feisty now and then as littermates try to find what works in the real world and what doesn't.

Just Cats

Just Cats

Exploring their brand new universe becomes the utmost priority to growing kittens. Cats are like sponges as they grow; carefully soaking up each and every drop of possible understanding as they examine their strange habitat and the people who scurry in and out of it. Kittens who receive tender, extra-sensitive care as they develop are able to trust and thoroughly enjoy human relationships for their entire lives. Savor the moments and treat that kitty well . . .

Kittens

. . . **f**or it's a short journey from kittenhood . . . to cat.

The months fly in a flurry of passionate discovery and zestful, high-spirited living. And the wonderful thing about kittens is that they don't stay that way! These darling, daring little devils mature in about a year's time to the steady, exquisite adult felines we know and love. Kittenness of course, is never fully shed in adult cats — and for this we are grateful. It just wouldn't do, to completely lose all that exuberant playfulness. Kitty mellows gradually and begins to transform into yet another grand and glorious feline. Long live the cat!